Anastasia's Journey

A Life of Prayer and God's Providence

A BIOGRAPHY OF

Anastasia Ioannidou Burr

Anastasia I. Burr

Published by
Whispering Pines Publishing
Shoals, IN

Printed by
Country Pines, Inc.
11013 Country Pines Road
Shoals, IN 47581

Contents

Foreword

God's Word tells us that without faith it is impossible to please God, Hebrews 11:6. To emphasize this truth and to give us examples of faith, this chapter further provides numerous accounts of faith exercised by many Old Testament saints as an encouragement to us to live by faith.

We can also gain perspectives on living by faith when we read accounts of the lives of more recent saints who lived by faith, such as Brother Lawrence, Madame Guyon, William Carey, Amy Carmichael, George Muller, and J. Edwin Orr to mention a few. Reading such accounts can be valuable in challenging us and instructing us in living our lives by faith as we see again God's faithfulness and providence in the lives of those who consistently trusted Him, to His praise and glory.

This book is another account of God's leading and provision in the life of one who lived a life of faith in trusting Him and following wherever He led her. Born Anastasia Ioannidou in a very humble Christian home in Greece, she trusted Jesus as her Savior and Lord at an early age. She trusted God for protection for her and her grandmother when the communists would repeatedly raid her village; she trusted God's leading and provision when she travelled to western Canada, without any resources, to get an education; she trusted God's leading and provision again when she went to London to go to nursing school; she trusted God when He led her to St. Luke's Hospital in Thessaloniki, Greece, when she had other interests; and she trusted Him when He led her to leave her profession, family, friends and country and move to the United States and marry Richard Burr, the President and Executive Director of Pray-Think-Act Ministries, Inc.

Now Anastasia is trusting God in what is often the greatest test of faith for God's people—suffering. For many years she has been afflicted with a rare disease of the brain called

5

frontal temporal degeneration ("FTD"). In her case it primarily affects her motor skills and environmental relational coping (her memory and thinking remain intact). She has spent the last seven years largely in bed with no interest in external stimuli such as books or television. Instead, she fills her time with praises, prayers and hymns. One day while visiting her I started to paraphrase Amy Carmichael, who was bedridden with pain for over twenty years in India. Amy said (again, I paraphrase) that trusting God in suffering was not merely enduring the suffering as His will—but before I could go on, Anastasia finished the thought!—that it is only in enduring it *with joy* that one is truly accepting His will and glorifying Him.

This is the unwavering faith and trust of Anastasia I. Burr in Jesus Christ, her Savior and Lord; and this book is another account of God's faithfulness in leading and providing for all needs in the life of one committed to Him and living out His will with joy wherever He leads. You will be encouraged as you are reminded again of God's faithfulness toward those who follow Him by faith, and challenged by another example of living by faith. May you be blessed by reading it, and may God be praised and glorified.

Stephen M. Westbrook
Chairman of the Board
Pray-Think-Act Ministries, Inc.

Acknowledgements

When the subject of writing the story of my life was first mentioned by our dear friends Pastor John and Marion Carlson in the early 1990's, I scoffed at such a thought in that my life was typical of any young girl growing up in Greece during the mid-forties and fifties. But John and Marion were very persistent, so I eventually said I'd pray about it, thinking that would diffuse such a notion. But from that conversation the Lord prompted me to begin writing in what eventually became *Anastasia's Poems.*

However, as the years passed, several other folk suggested similar nonsense and finally Richard became more resolute, insisting that such a book would be glorifying to God and by His direction it could be of much encouragement to believers both near and far. Included in this chorus of enthusiasts were two university professors, with one of them offering to write the book with the condition of anonymity. After much resistance we agreed. She then prepared a detailed outline of questions in which Richard was the interviewer collecting several hours of material; and then our anonymous author, and dearest friend, researched and wrote the manuscript you hold in your hands.

I am deeply humbled and thankful to our sovereign Lord for raising up such a gifted sister of the faith to bring this project to fruition. May His name be venerated, His kingdom expanded and His purposes accomplished. To our Triune God be all glory!

Anastasia Ioannidou Burr

CHAPTER 1

The Early Years

Four-year-old Anastasia made her way across the quiet sitting room and climbed onto her Grandmother's welcoming lap. It was time to pray and Grandmother was already kneeling on the homemade rugs spread over the straw that covered their mud floor. Mother, Father, and all of Anastasia's siblings had slipped out and were on their way to Giannitsa, the nearest city, where they would be safe for the night. In the morning they would make the 5-mile trip back to their small Greek village for another day of work and school. Communist soldiers weren't interested in little girls and elderly women so Anastasia felt safe as she snuggled into Grandmother's lap and drew comfort from her familiar voice. The beautiful Turkish words seemed to flow effortlessly from her lips as she interceded aloud and with great passion for her beloved country, asking God to defeat the Communists and bring an end to their brutal oppression.

The Greek Civil War brought with it the forced enlistment of men, women, and youth that terrorized villages like Neos Mylotopos, the small farming community in northern Greece where Anastasia lived with her family. After hiding in the mountains all day, the Communist soldiers entered the villages at night and went door-to-door demanding food. Anastasia's family initially complied, surrendering bread and other staples in response to the soldiers' demands, but, like their neighbors, they were frightened by the recruitment process and the prospect of being taken away to the mountains where they would be trained in Communist ideology. The threat was real; the Communists killed those who disagreed with them.

Those years of nightly separation and retreat to Giannitsa were difficult for the Ioannidou family, but the hours spent alone with Grandmother at home laid a strong foundation for little Anastasia, a foundation of prayer and deep trust in the providence of God. Grandmother ended her day at the throne of grace and returned at dawn with her Bible open, a pattern that Anastasia would adopt as her own and that would sustain her through every phase of life.

The Ioananidous were a large hardworking family that was rich in love and faith, tracing their spiritual roots back to the Ottoman Empire. American missionaries were working among the Greeks in Turkey during the late 1800s and early 1900s, a period of time when both Christianity and missionaries were tolerated, and it was then that the Gospel first reached Anastasia's family. Anastasia's grandmother, Sultana, was born in 1887 in the city of Adana in southern Turkey and came to know Christ as a young woman.

Sultana later married Ignatius, also a native of Adana. He was 15 years her senior and did not know the Lord. In 1913, shortly after the birth of their first child Lydia, the couple found their young family caught up in a national crisis. The Ottoman Empire was in chaos and began to conscript Greek residents into the army to engage in the systematic elimination of fellow Greeks who were of the Christian-Ottoman Greek population in Anatolia and also for what would be known as the Armenian massacre, an act of genocide that exterminated approximately 1.5 million people between 1910-1915. Many of the Greeks living in Turkey had been taken there forcibly as a result of previous military conflicts; now the government was converting their descendants into soldiers who would be forced to risk their own lives and commit atrocious acts of violence on behalf of the Empire.

Though many Ottoman Greeks did become pawns in the hands of the Empire, Anastasia's ancestors went to great lengths to avoid conscription. After government officials attempted to draft him, her grandfather Ignatius realized that his only hope was to leave the country. At 40 years old, he left behind his young wife Sultana to raise their baby girl alone and traveled under the cover of darkness from Adana to Constantinople, modern day Istanbul. He boarded a ship, the *Ar-*

gentina, and escaped from Turkey along with 11 other Greek compatriots. One of his traveling companions was a young man named Christos who, in desperation to avoid conscription and travel with the crew to America, lied to the ship's captain and claimed to be 21 rather than 17 years old.

By the grace of God, the *Argentina* carried them safely to the shores of the United States where they disembarked at Ellis Island. Their plan was to work hard, earn as much money as possible and return to their families as soon as they could. The group was separated, and the men scattered throughout the northern states with some taking jobs at coal mines in Pennsylvania and West Virginia and others working for the railroad in Wisconsin. The work was physically demanding and at times even dangerous, but they labored wholeheartedly in anticipation of being reunited with their loved ones.

Several years passed, and in 1923 the Ottoman Empire collapsed entirely. Turkey sent the Greeks home to resettle, and the Greek government gave them land on which they could build homes and start small farms for income to sustain their families. Sultana and her daughter Lydia moved to Neos Mylotopos. Though Greek in heritage, they had never lived outside of Turkey and were blessed to be able to relocate along with their Turkish church family, a group of 60-65 people. At the same time on the other side of the Atlantic, after working in the United States for 13 years, Christos, now a grown man, left America and returned to Greece as well. Upon his arrival, he sought out Ignatius' family and spent considerable time with them, especially their teenage daughter. In 1927, Christos married 14-year-old Lydia, much to the displeasure of her father. In fact, Ignatius was so upset that he decided to stay in the United States and consequently cut off all communication with his family. The emotional pain of their physical separation, which had already lasted more than a decade, was now heightened by Ignatius' termination of all correspondence. Sultana and her family prayed fervently that he would return.

Meanwhile, Christos and Lydia started a family and their humble home burst at the seams with both love and children. Over the course of several years, they welcomed three boys

11

and three girls. Nicos was the firstborn, Constantine arrived in 1932, Alice in 1933 and Evangeline in 1934. George was the fifth child and Anastasia the last, entering the world on January 11, 1944. (Two of the children, Nicos and George, died before Anastasia was born, and their birthdates are unknown to the remaining family members.)

The small house, occupying approximately 700 square feet, was practical in design, and was built out of mud bricks that the family had fashioned by hand. Big, red ceramic tiles lined the roof. The house was rectangular in shape and consisted of 3 rooms. At one end was the sitting room or living area that also served as sleeping quarters for all seven family members who shared the house when Anastasia was a young girl. Mother and Father shared one of the double beds and Anastasia and her sister Alice shared the other. Evangeline bunked in another very small bed and Grandmother bedded down every night on a homemade, wool-stuffed mattress that she placed on the floor near the heating stove. Constantine, the only boy at home, fended for himself. The mud floor was overlaid with straw rugs, which in turn, were covered with regular rugs, some that Grandmother had made by hand on a loom.

Their kitchen, the second room in the middle of the rectangular structure, held a fireplace where Lydia and her daughters cooked meals. They also availed themselves of a large outdoor oven, built of stone and bricks and lined with smooth cement, for baking delicious spinach and feta cheese pies, 10 to 12 big loaves of bread at a time, and even cookies. The mud floor in the kitchen had been leveled and dried. There was no heat, electricity, or running water, so multiple times throughout the day, one of the Ioannidou women made her way to the well outside, turned the crank to lower the bucket attached by rope, and hauled up the heavy load of water that was so crucial for cooking, washing and housekeeping. Given the lack of running water, bathroom facilities were a small outhouse in the yard.

On the other side of the kitchen, the third and final room served as a barn to shelter the family's two cows, two horses and one goat. In one corner was a chicken coop with an open-

Anastasia's grandmother, Sultana, is in the center. To her left is Anastasia's mother, Lydia (age 12). This picture was taken in 1923 when they arrived in Greece from Turkey.

ing to the outdoors; the birds were protected at night from predators but free to roam outside all day.

Christos owned 37 Greek acres, the equivalent of approximately eight acres in the United States. He was a quiet man who modeled a strong work ethic and supported his family by raising corn, wheat, and cotton. It was hard work, and everyone who was old enough pitched in to help. In fact, Grandmother Sultana, in spite of her physical disabilities, having been born with a dislocated hip that was never treated, was the best cotton picker of all! They also cared for eight to ten beehives that provided a delicious year-round supply of honey.

Life in Mylotopos, with a population of approximately 2,000, had always revolved around agriculture, and villagers' strong sense of community life was evident in numerous ways. Rather than live on their own land, farmers preferred to travel daily to their fields and return each evening to their homes in the village where they could live side by side with their neighbors, a pattern that still characterizes village life today. Their close-knit community provided a warm, safe environment for families with children, and Anastasia spent leisurely summer days playing games outdoors with friends and looked forward in the evenings to visits from neighbors or relatives who stopped in for coffee.

Even as they became more established and had the financial resources to build a bigger house, the Ioannidou family continued to open their doors in warm hospitality. When Anastasia was about ten years old, her family constructed a two-story house with a second floor that was big enough for three bedrooms, a large living room, a kitchen and a bathroom. They still used an outhouse but installed the bathroom in anticipation that villagers would one day have access to indoor plumbing, a dream that became reality when Anastasia was 15. Guests frequently gathered for coffee in the new, more spacious kitchen, but the Ioannidous were not wealthy and had to be good stewards of all that they had. One particular evening, Christos expressed frustration over the frequency with which his wife and daughters broke coffee cups when they accidentally dropped them in the hard mosaic sink and declared that this particular night he would wash the dishes himself. He successfully crossed the kitchen with one cup in hand, but a sudden stumble sent it tumbling into the sink where it shattered into tiny pieces. He turned bright red with embarrassment but couldn't help joining in the hearty laughter of his friends and family.

Unlike their Orthodox neighbors, Anastasia's family was actively involved in the Greek Evangelical Church, a community of dedicated believers that make up less than 1% of Greece's population. Though relationships in Mylotopos were friendly, the Orthodox majority regarded the Evangelicals as heretics, and this difference in religious belief produced occasional conflict. One Monday morning at her elementary school, Anastasia, a sixth grader, and four or five other children were called into one of the teacher's offices. He was a tall, unpleasant man, and the children immediately felt afraid as they looked up at his towering figure. He grilled them about their absence from the orthodox service on Sunday and was even more displeased when they replied that they had attended their own. In response, he ordered them to hold out their palms and proceeded to strike each child very forcefully on the hand with a stick. The children reported this punishment to their parents, who were very upset, and news of the incident spread quickly throughout their evangelical circle. Their pastor paid a visit to the teacher in which he insisted on the legitimacy of their church and demanded that the children be left alone.

Anastasia was an excellent student, though according to an oft-repeated family anecdote, got off to a rather unenthusiastic start in school. There was no kindergarten program, so first grade marked her entrance into academia. After taking Anastasia to school on that all-important first day, Lydia was surprised to see her daughter walk quietly back into the house just a few short hours later. Anastasia had left during the first recess and offered a simple explanation: "I don't know how to read and write, so I can't go to school." Mother took her by the hand and responded, "That's precisely why you are supposed to be there" and marched her daughter directly back to the classroom.

Anastasia was particularly gifted in the area of languages. Her father had learned a bit of English during his time in the United States and taught her some vocabulary as well as how to count from one to ten. His use of English seeded a love in her heart for America and for language. Every time she returned from school having earned a ten on an assignment, the equivalent of an A in the United States, she would call out to him, "Patéras, Patéras! (Father, Father!)" as she approached the house, and once she got his attention would exclaim loudly in English "Ten, Ten"!

Though they were hardworking members of the community, faithful in church attendance, and sincere in their religious devotion, the majority of Anastasia's family, with the exception of Grandmother Sultana, was not actually born again. Lydia served as the spiritual leader of the home and constantly thanked the Lord for His provisions for the family. Christos, who had been Orthodox for the first ten years of his married life, often demanded that she attend the Orthodox Church as well, but Lydia consistently refused. The devotion of this deeply religious family was about to be transformed by the powerful message of the Gospel when an Australian evangelist arrived in the village.

Anastasia (age 10) holding her cousin, Frieda, in her front yard.

The members of Anastasia's church gathered nightly to hear the visiting preacher during two weeks of meetings. He explained that our forefathers Adam and Eve were created to enjoyed intimate fellowship with God in the Garden of Eden, but that their perfect world was destroyed when they questioned the goodness of God and disobeyed Him. Their sin created an impenetrable barrier between them and God that resulted in immediate expulsion from the garden and ultimate physical and spiritual death. The tragic consequences of their sin would rest on every single one of their descendants; every human being is now tainted by sin at birth and rather than experiencing the kind of sweet fellowship with God that He originally intended, is instead His enemy. The evangelist went on to explain that out of His deep love, God implemented a wonderful plan to restore His broken relationship with this fallen world. He would send His Son Jesus, the perfectly Holy Son of God, would take on the nature of a mere human and be born as a little baby to a virgin mother. He would grow up to be a man who would display the glory of God by proclaiming the sin of humankind and contrasting it with the love of God, by doing miraculous deeds, and by showing how our relationship to God the Father could be restored. This sinless Son was condemned as a sinner by His own creation and hung on a cross to die in our place. He was buried in a tomb, but on the third day, rose victoriously from the grave and with that resurrection conquered the power of sin and of death. To as many as receive Him by acknowledging their own sin and unworthiness, accepting His death on their behalf, repenting from sin, and completely surrendering their lives to the Lord Jesus Christ, God offers forgiveness. That forgiveness means fellowship with Him now and the promise of life eternal with Him in the future. The power of this Good News, this Gospel message, penetrated the hearts of those present in a powerful way, and Lydia, Anastasia's mother, gave her heart to Christ as did her oldest sister Alice.

Seated together with the other children in the church building, nine-year-old Anastasia listened to the preacher with rapt attention and felt the Lord speaking to her heart. She knew that she was a sinner and had a deep sense of conviction but at that time there was no one present to follow up with the children and address their spiritual needs. Anastasia never forgot that message, however, and the seeds of truth that were sown in her heart that evening would grow over time and soon bear fruit.

Once Anastasia completed elementary school, she attended grades 7-9 in nearby Ginnatisa, but she studied her last three years of high school in Katerini, a larger city of about 40,000 people. It was almost 2 hours by bus from Mylotopos, so her sister Alice, who had married a man from Katerini and relocated there, invited Anastasia to stay with them. Because classes met 6 days a week, traveling home on the weekend was not possible, and Anastasia was only able to return home at Easter, Christmas and during the summer break. For a young teenage girl, it was very difficult to be separated from her parents, and she looked forward with eager anticipation to her mother's visits, though they were necessarily infrequent.

While in Katerini, Anastasia attended a large Evangelical church and in the spring of 1959 participated in two weeks of evangelistic meetings conducted by the pastor. She wept over her sin as she sat through those evening meetings and on an evening that she will never forget, March 26, 1959, gave her life to Jesus by repenting and anchoring her faith in Him. Anastasia was a changed young woman. She had been dead in her sins but was awakened to newness of life by the Spirit of Christ. She was now a new creation with a new attitude and a new vision for her future. During that unforgettable week, they watched a film about 5 young missionaries who had been killed in 1956 by the Aucas, an indigenous group in Ecuador with whom they had hoped to share the gospel. Elisabeth Eliot, one of the missionary widows, recounts the whole story in her book, Through Gates of Splendor. Anastasia wept as she watched the movie and sensed that God was calling her, too, to be a missionary, specifically a missionary nurse. She accepted that call and, as a girl of only 15, offered up the first of many prayers that God would lead her wherever He wanted. She belonged to Jesus now and had begun a lifelong journey of prayer and trust in the Providence of God.

The Gospel had yet to penetrate the heart of each family member, but Grandmother Sultana, Lydia and the children continued to pray, and those years of faithful intercession bore much fruit and brought about an amazing and clearly providential turn of events. Many years later in 1971, an unexpected visitor showed up one day at Anastasia's home in Mylotopos. He was Greek but had been living in America, and he came bearing incredible news. Grandfather Ignatius was alive! The family was shocked. They had prayed for years and years that God would save their grandfather and bring him home to meet the grandchildren he had never known. The visitor told Sultana that Ignatius was living in Massillon, Ohio, where he was receiving a pension from the government for all his years of work in the mines and on the railroad but warned them that he was not well. He was an alcoholic and his life was in ruins. Constantine, the eldest son, took responsibility for investigating these claims and set off for the United States. Not knowing what awaited him, he made his way to Massillon and, after consulting with contacts in the area, was able to track down his grandfather's whereabouts. Ignatius was living in an old, run-down tenement. At 100 years old, his mind was still remarkably sharp, but his body had become as filthy and unkempt as his surroundings. One can only imagine the shock this poor, lonely man felt when Constantine arrived at his house and said, "I'm your grandson," urging him with open arms to come home. It was time for the prodigal to return. He had rejected his family, but they had not rejected him. And so, bathed and scrubbed and dressed in fresh, clean clothes, Ignatius boarded a plane for Thessaloniki in the care of the loving grandson he had just met for the first time.

Grandfather was greeted at the airport by the most enthusiastic welcome committee one could imagine. Tears flowed freely as he fell into the waiting arms of his two younger brothers and was introduced one by one to the grandchildren and great-grandchildren he had never met. He was welcomed into the home of his now 60-year-old daughter and her husband and was sweetly reunited with his devoted wife, Sultana. People came from near and far to see with their own eyes the wonder of this old man who had returned to his family after six decades of estrangement.

As the days passed, Ignatius was wracked with guilt over his waywardness and the terrible pain he had caused by abandoning his family. His daughter spoke with him in Turkish telling him day after day of the love of God. Ignatius finally asked, "How can you forgive me for what I've done to you?" Lydia replied, "We can forgive you because our sins have been forgiven by the blood of Jesus Christ. God's Son died on the cross to take away our sin, and He puts love in our hearts. That's what makes us love you. We're so glad you're with us." God used a loving family and words of truth about Jesus to crack open a heart that had been hardened by 100 years of rebellion, and after just three weeks at home, Grandfather dropped to his knees and prayed: "Take me, O God, and put me in the arms of your Son. I'm sorry for what I've done and the life that I've lived that was not according to your will." It was a simple prayer from a broken man with a repentant heart. God honored that prayer, and Ignatius was forever changed. He savored the forgiveness of his God and his family and led a happy, transformed life until the Lord called him home at the age of 107. Anastasia would never forget the example of her grandmother's persistent intercession nor the miraculous reunion the providence of God had granted to their family after 60 years of pleading on behalf of their prodigal grandfather.

About the time of Grandfather's return and after years of attending the evangelical church, Anastasia's father, Christos, also accepted Christ as his personal Savior. Constantine, her brother, accepted the Lord as an adult as well, giving his 40-year-old heart to the Savior while attending a Christian conference. Evangeline was the last to surrender her life and accepted Christ in 1991. During that season, she had the privilege of caring for her elderly mother, Lydia, who at the age of 78 was dying. Evangeline observed as Lydia spoke all day long with her dear friend Jesus and was so moved by her faith that she collapsed into her mother's arms and declared through tears, "I am confessing today my sins to Christ, and I want to become His child, and I want you to know that I will see you in heaven."

These moving stories of conversion were interspersed with several very painful family tragedies. Little George died from complications of the measles at the tender age of two, a loss that brought tremendous heartache. They were also devastated by the sudden passing of their oldest son, Nicos, who became ill at the age of 16 and died within 24 hours from a burst appendix. Lydia was inconsolable until one night when the Father of mercies and God of all comfort ministered to her in a very personal way. She dreamed that she was weeping at Nicos' grave when an angel dressed in white appeared to her and said, "Why are you weeping? Your son is with Jesus." The reassurance of her son's eternal life in Christ comforted her deeply, and she never again mourned with the same intensity.

Through tragedy and triumph, Anastasia witnessed first-hand the power of prayer and saw the providence of God woven throughout the fabric of her family life. He had blessed them with great joy and they were far more conscious of His gracious provision than of their financial limitations. This strong foundation would serve her well as she prepared to launch out on her own.

CHAPTER 2

Preparing for Service

When Anastasia completed her high school education in 1962, she was as committed as ever to the call to missionary service that she had received at the evangelistic meetings just a few years prior. She decided to stay in Greece for one additional year to study English intensively at a language institute. Her love for the language, cultivated in part by her father, continued to grow, and studying was a pleasure. At the same time, God was preparing her heart and mind for the next step: a move to Canada.

She had heard very good reports from several acquaintances about Millar Memorial Bible Institute (now Millar College of the Bible) in Pambrun, Saskatchewan, and felt that the Lord was prompting her to study there as well. She contacted a missionary alumnus who, by God's providence, was attending a Christian conference in Greece. The whole admissions process advanced very quickly and, before she knew it, the young village girl who had never been more than 100 miles from home was starting a new life across the Atlantic. At 19 years of age, she boarded her first airplane en route to Brussels. From there she flew to Montreal where a family she knew from Greece met her at the airport and graciously took her into their home to rest for three days before getting her settled on the train for a long ride across Canada.

The route took her through four provinces: Quebec, Ontario, Manitoba and finally Saskatchewan. It was March 1963, and Anastasia was traveling through a veritable winter wonderland. She had never seen so much snow in her life! The train stopped in every little village along the way making a long journey even longer and giving her much time to ponder the miraculous provision of God for this new adventure. Her parents had been able to pay for her airfare and travel expenses but did not have the financial resources to cover the other costs of her education. The Institute, however, had found a couple that was willing to support her by paying her tuition as well as room and board.

The train finally pulled into the station at Pambrun where a faculty member from the Institute was awaiting Anastasia's arrival. She climbed off the train wondering if she had reached the end of the earth. The school was located in a very small rural community in the heart of the Canadian prairie, and stretching out before her, as far as her eye could see, were what seemed to be never ending fields of wheat. It was a far cry from the bustling community life of Greece, particularly the last few years she had spent in a larger city, but she had arrived at last, and God's call for her to be a missionary nurse was beginning to take shape.

It was a very small school with only 120 students, but both peers and college personnel accepted Anastasia with open arms, and she developed meaningful relationships with many of them. When they struggled to pronounce her name, she proposed "Tessie" as an alternative, and it stuck. She was not able to go home during the four years she spent in Canada, so the invitations from faculty to their homes for dinner and holiday celebrations were very special. She spent her first summer in a nearby city where she babysat two small girls in exchange for room and board and $40 a month. The second summer she stayed on campus to paint and clean with four or five other students; they were not paid, but their work was credited toward tuition costs. And her third summer was spent at the home of the campus maintenance person and his family who graciously took her in. She had no regular income, but the Lord gave her the faith to trust that He would provide, often through her brothers and sisters in Christ. At times after lunch she returned to the coat rack hanging outside the dining room to find a wad of money tucked into one of her pockets. The Lord met "Tessie's" every need.

Anastasia took courses on the Bible, church history, and missions. Her professors were godly examples and helpful teachers. She was an excellent student and attributed her strong academic performance not to her own intelligence or work ethic but to the grace of God. One particularly memorable assignment, especially for a student like Anastasia who spoke English as a second language, was from Dr. Peeler's evangelism class. He assigned 100 Bible verses that students had to commit to memory and required that they demonstrate their mastery of the material through a very specific and challenging exam; they had to quote every verse for which he gave a reference and, vice versa, provide the reference for every verse he supplied. Dr. Peeler had been an evangelist and was a graduate of Moose Jaw Bible College before it relocated to Pambrun and was renamed after Dr. William J. Millar. He was left to direct the school after Dr. Millar's sudden passing and served in leadership there for over five decades. Years later when Anastasia returned to Canada, she had an opportunity to visit this godly man whom she held in the highest regard.

Anastasia with Dr. Peeler in the early 90's, who was president of Millar Memorial Bible Institute when she was a student.

The first year presented the greatest challenge to her English skills, and God provided extra support through another special person, Ms. Helen Dickson. Her father had been a co-founder of the school, and her sister was married to the current professor and president, Dr. Peeler. Ms. Dickson was like a mother to Anastasia. She helped her with English, invited her home for holidays, and invested in her spiritual wellbeing.

During her years in Bible school, Anastasia felt that God was calling her to serve as a missionary in Persia, modern-day Iran, a country that was closed to religious workers but not to professionals like doctors and nurses. Toward the end of her third year, Dr. Spiros Zodhiates, a Greek American Bible scholar, was the speaker at a conference hosted at her school. Given their common cultural background, he was particularly interested to meet Anastasia and when he asked about her future plans, she shared her thoughts about Persia. He responded with a surprising retort, "What?! Persia?! Don't tell me that. You're going back to Greece." Somewhat stunned, Anastasia listened carefully as he continued, "We're going to build a hospital in Greece and are going to need Christian doctors and nurses. Pray about this and see if the Lord doesn't want you to go back to Greece and become a part of this ministry."

Anastasia made the matter the focus of very concentrated prayer and soon came to the conclusion that the Lord was indeed calling her back to Greece. Her years at Bible school in Canada, immersed in the study of God's word and living in community with godly mentors and fellow students, were the best years of her life. She was learning firsthand how her Heavenly Father moved in response to the heartfelt prayers of His children and, as she advanced to the next phase of preparation for missionary service, she would continue to trace the providence of God in every detail of her life.

It was now 1968 and Anastasia had completed the three-year program of study at Millar. She traveled to Boston where her sister Alice and her husband were living and sought admission to a nursing program there. She passed the required test of general knowledge but was not accepted because she did not have a high school diploma from the United States.

As she journeyed back to Saskatchewan where she could pray and seek direction about her next step, Anastasia was not yet aware of the divine appointment that awaited her.

During her absence, another young Greek woman, Salome Anastasiadou, had come to study the Bible at Millar in preparation for serving as a medical missionary in Latin America. They had met years earlier when Anastasia was living in Katerini and were happy to be reacquainted, but when Anastasia left Greece for Canada, this young woman had gone to London where she studied nursing in a Christian facility, Mildmay Mission Hospital. The two women developed a special friendship during their brief time together at Millar, and the Lord used this renewed relationship to convince Anastasia that God was calling her to a nursing program in London, not in the United States.

After those additional three months at Millar, Anastasia returned home to spend a year with her mother and father, both of whom she had missed terribly during her time away at school. From Greece she could care for her parents and correspond with Mildmay about the possibility of studying there. Mildmay's origins trace back to the mid 1860s when the Reverend William Pennefather and his wife Catherine spearheaded efforts to care for victims of a serious cholera epidemic in the worst slums of London's East End. Their concern for both the physical and spiritual needs of the poor expanded, and Mildmay Mission Hospital opened in 1892 with 27 beds, one doctor, a handful of nurses, and several deaconesses in training. The hospital served East London for nearly 100 years until it was closed in 1982, but it reopened just a few years later in 1988 as the first hospice in Europe for individuals suffering from AIDS-related ailments.

In 1969 at the age of 25 Anastasia boarded a London-bound plane from Athens and embarked on the next stage of her preparation for missionary service. She had never been in London before and arriving in such a huge, bustling city would have been even more overwhelming were it not for the personal welcome she received at the airport. Her host hailed a cab and took her, along with all her luggage, to the dormitory that would be her home for the next several years. When the supervisor left her in her room to settle in, Anastasia was immediately struck with pangs of sadness. She realized that her new environment and experience would be very different from Pambrun, but classes were soon to begin and there would be little time for homesickness or nostalgia.

It was an intense program with no summer break, but each nurse received 15 days of vacation that Anastasia used for traveling to Greece, sometimes via multiple flights across Europe and other times by means of a 48-hour train ride. Tuition, along with room and board, were free, and the nursing students were given a small stipend for spending money from which Anastasia saved money for her trips home. The nursing students followed a cycle that consisted of 15 days of classroom instruction at the Royal London Hospital followed by 2 months in the clinical wards at Mildmay to apply what they had learned. The human body was fascinating, and she found herself increasingly awed by the wisdom of the Creator who had designed it. The nursing students had little contact with physicians at this time, but the instructors were competent and supportive. For Anastasia, learning the terminology for body parts, procedures, illnesses, and medications in English was almost like learning a new language, but her native Greek skills coupled with four years of high school Latin proved invaluable and gave her a considerable advantage. She did well on her exams, enjoyed all that she was learning, and performed very well as a student.

Nursing was a challenging profession both intellectually and practically. It was not easy to understand the wide variety of illnesses with which the patients presented and to grasp the details of their diagnoses. On the practical side, some patients were very hard to love, yet it was the nurses' responsibility to treat them well and give them the best care possible. They monitored each one thoroughly and immediately reported anything unusual to the head nurse or to a doctor. Bathing the bed-ridden twice a week was physically demanding but even more difficult was the emotional toll of losing a patient. Anastasia felt the heartache of bereft family members and soon learned how to communicate effectively with them in their grief. Preparing the body of a deceased patient for the mortician was a vivid reminder of human mortality and the urgency of the Gospel message. For some reason, patients often died during the night, adding a layer of literal darkness to the figurative valley of the shadow of death.

Outside the hospital these were also years of personal and spiritual growth. Though she had limited free time, Anastasia developed a special friendship with two fellow nursing students, Kirsti Soromies of Finland and Youna Doss from Egypt. They shared, prayed, and attended worship services together. She also had girlfriends with whom she visited the stores in London to shop for clothes and shoes and to admire the beautiful English bone china. Now in her mid-twenties, Anastasia was interested in dating, but no opportunity for courtship presented itself, and she continued interacting primarily with her female classmates and companions.

Her spiritual life was interwoven with her hospital training. All the hospital staff were believers and as a community they encouraged one another in their individual journeys of faith. At 9am every morning the nurses took turns giving devotions over the hospital's intercom system that was funneled into all the patients' rooms, and at 8pm every evening those nurses on overnight duty gathered in a prayer room to intercede for their patients and for the night shift who would be serving them. On Thursday nights at the hospital Anastasia and her colleagues attended a Bible study hosted by Nurses Christian Fellowship, and a second weekly gathering was open to all hospital staff and to any unbelieving friends they wanted to invite.

Opportunities for spiritual encouragement and growth at Mildmay included both community gatherings for study and fellowship as well as deep personal relationships. Audrey Patterson was one particularly remarkable woman who had a profound impact on Anastasia during this season of life. She was Jamaican and had moved to London for work. Passersby may have mistaken her for a mere cleaning lady, but those who met her immediately sensed her vibrant relationship with the Lord. She used washing and dusting and sweeping as a platform for ministry and did not miss a single opportunity to speak words of Scripture to the nurses or leave Bible verses on their tables. Anastasia was deeply blessed by her friendship and kept in contact with her for decades.

On most Sundays Anastasia had the privilege of attending services at area evangelical churches like Westminster Chapel, where Dr. Martin Lloyd-Jones had preached. She was blessed by the sound Biblical teaching, and it was at Westminster that she was fully exposed to reformed theology with its focus on the sovereignty of God. Her understanding of theology was shaped by that emphasis and she began reading her Bible, specifically passages about Jesus choosing His disciples and calling sinners, through that lens.

More than ten years had passed since she gave her life to Christ and felt his call to be a missionary, and now in 1973, at the age of 29, Anastasia completed her preparation at Mildmay and was officially trained a registered nurse. The Lord had answered every prayer and had guided her across thousands of miles by plane, train and automobile. He had enabled her to learn English, adapt to two new cultures, pay every bill, and pass every exam. He blessed her with friendships grounded in Christ, and she would enter the nursing profession with a deep understanding of His Word and His ways. Anastasia had learned firsthand that the great God to whom her grandmother had prayed for deliverance from the Communists years before was absolutely faithful, and she could now trace his providential leading in the broadest strokes and in the smallest details of her life.

After much prayer, Anastasia was certain that God had called her to serve Him in Greece. In preparation, she stayed in London through 1974 for further study in the Intensive Care Unit and traveled briefly to Boston in 1975 where she took a special course in Psychiatric Nurses Training at Massachusetts General Hospital. She then returned to her homeland to become the one of the first nurses at St. Luke's Hospital in Thessaloniki.

CHAPTER 3

Missionary Nurse

St. Luke's Hospital was founded in 1975 with the goal of providing excellent medical care for the Greek people and, at the same time, sharing with them the Good News of Jesus Christ. It opened with 180 beds and only five or six nurses. By the grace of God and the hard work of its medical personnel, it quickly earned an excellent reputation, and even in its early days was regarded by doctors as an oasis from the state-run hospitals in Thessaloniki. Since then, St. Luke's has grown to a 270-bed facility with a staff of over 500 that serves more than 2,000 patients in a given month.

Anastasia arrived in October 1975 to set about the demanding, yet rewarding, work of nursing. She began her career at St. Luke's as a Registered Nurse and was head of a ward whose patients suffered from a wide variety of ailments, some requiring medical and some surgical intervention. The most enjoyable and challenging aspect of her work was evangelism, and she vividly remembers the first patient she led to Christ.

A young 24-year-old communist university student had been admitted to the hospital with colon cancer. The staff shared with him a great deal about his spiritual need, but he did not respond. One morning, Anastasia was paged over the intercom and recognized the room number to which she was being sent as belonging to the university student for whom they had prayed incessantly and to whom they had spoken about Jesus so many times. Little did she know, that just a few moments earlier, this weak young man had told the director of the hospital that he saw a chasm before him and that it was impassable. He readily accepted the director's offer to send someone to speak with him.

When Anastasia arrived and asked what he needed, the young man replied, "I want to receive Christ as my Savior." He told Anastasia about the impassable chasm and indicated that He felt the need to know God and His Son Jesus Christ. She sat down at his side and, through tears, prayed a simple prayer that he repeated phrase by phrase after her. When they finished, Anastasia opened her eyes to a young man beaming with joy who began to speak of the incredible weight off his back and the fear that had disappeared. Just as she rose to leave, the patient's mother entered the room. Unable to contain himself, the young man burst out, "Mother, I've just accepted Jesus in my heart. He's my Savior and I will be able to pass this chasm that I feel. You need to do the same thing."

Anastasia left the room ecstatic and ran downstairs to share the exciting news with the director, but before she reached his office, much to her surprise, she ran into Dr. Spiros Zodhiates who was just arriving at the hospital. This dear servant of God, the very man who had counseled her years before that she should serve as a missionary nurse in Greece rather than Persia, was the first person with whom she was privileged to share that the first patient at St. Luke's had come to Christ. It was a beautiful glimpse into the mysterious ways of God: the divine intertwining of His children's paths that morning confirmed that He had answered their prayers offered up years before in Canada and that they were in the center of His will. The hospital staff rejoiced along with the angels in Heaven over this young sinner who had repented.

Those laboring in the mission fields of Greece, however, found themselves in one of Europe's most challenging countries. Yes, patients came to Christ but not in droves. The Greek were Orthodox, and little had changed since Anastasia was a small girl in Mylotopos; they believed that their baptism as infants made them Christians and that they could reach heaven by performing good works and devotedly following church traditions.

Most patients were opposed to any other religion, and some were truly hostile to Evangelical Christianity. For them it did not rise above the status of a cult or heresy. Staff at the

Above: Anastasia is on the right, age 35, Director of Nursing at St. Luke's Hospital in Thessaloniki, Greece. Her cousin, Frieda, is on the left. Below: Anastasia (age 35) is on the left and her mother, Lydia, is in the center.

hospital, however, placed a New Testament beside each bed, and because patients were accustomed to their priests reading to them from the Bible, many were open to the nurses reading with them as well. Only the Lord could change hearts.

After a year in the ward, Anastasia was offered a position as the Director of Nursing, a challenging opportunity that she eagerly accepted. Because nursing was not considered a prestigious vocation in Greece, and many parents discouraged their daughters from pursuing it, there was a shortage of nurses. Consequently, the hospital had to employ nurses' aides to fulfill many duties that would be typically performed by a registered nurse. As Director of Nursing, Anastasia played a role in teaching aides to perform a variety of tasks, ranging from simple chores such as making beds to the very specific procedures involved in changing dressings and giving injections. At times she felt the weight of her supervisory responsibility and was apprehensive about the possibility of aides making life-threatening mistakes such as dispensing an incorrect medication. But, by the grace of God, there were no serious incidents, and the hospital staff at all levels went about their work with great care.

Anastasia's administrative role demanded a great deal of time. It was her responsibility to fill in when aides were unable to perform certain duties or left for home without finishing all their assigned tasks. She worked 11-hour days on average, but her shift could extend up to 20 hours when she was in the intensive care unit. On many Saturday evenings she traveled to Mylotopos to visit family and returned back to her apartment in Thessaloniki on Sunday evenings. The trip was tiring and took several hours each way, but it was always wonderful to be with her family. Nevertheless, after a time, the weight of her responsibilities and long hours at the hospital began to take a physical and spiritual toll, and, as she grew more tired, Anastasia became lax about spending time with the Lord each morning before going to work. Eventually, this lack of prayer and Scripture study resulted in a spiritual dullness and a distance from God. Her busyness led to barrenness.

Just as the Lord ministered to his exhausted servant Elijah

in the Old Testament, he intervened on Anastasia's behalf as well. She accepted an invitation to attend a Christian conference for nurses and hospital workers and traveled to Holland where she enjoyed fellowship with about 20 other medical personnel from all across Europe. Two dear ladies, both of them former nurses, provided the teaching and by the third day, Anastasia felt the Lord at work, answering her prayer for a revival in her heart. In addition to the weight of her missionary work, she had been struggling with some personal burdens as well. A 35-year-old single woman, she was concerned about marriage. The Lord had not provided a husband, but the revival that flooded her heart assured her that God had a good plan for her life and she began to experience peace that passed all understanding. He took away her burden about being single so fully that she no longer cared whether or not she married. Her communion with God was so real and powerful that tears of joy rolled down her cheek as she prayed. By the end of the conference, she was stronger both physically and spiritually and had never felt so happy and close to the Lord, singing in her heart and trusting Him with all of her soul.

When Anastasia returned to St. Luke's, her colleagues noticed immediately that she was a different person, and she had the opportunity to share her experience with the Christian nurses. Her personal revival did not end as she resumed her professional responsibilities and, in fact, birthed a new excitement about sharing the Gospel with her patients. One particular opportunity was especially memorable. A patient we will refer to as Mrs. P. was the wife of a military general; she struggled emotionally in a difficult marriage and physically with a cardiac problem that was expected to take her life. Her personal pain and medical condition led to desperation, and she constantly crossed herself calling out to Mary the mother of Jesus, to saints, and to God. The day before she died, Anastasia went to visit her early in the morning and heard her exclaim yet again, "Oh Mother of Jesus, have mercy on me. Oh God, have mercy on me." Anastasia very gently interjected, "Mrs. P., which one died for you—the Mother of Jesus or Jesus Himself?" The patient responded, "Jesus of course." "Well then," replied Anastasia, "to whom should you be praying?" And, Mrs. P. immediately started praying, "Oh Jesus, have mercy on me. I have been a sinner. Forgive me and take me to your presence." Anastasia left that room weeping with joy and told everyone that their dear patient had prayed the sinner's prayer. It was indeed a rich time of ministry for all the doctors and nurses, and they saw the Lord's hand at work, rewarding their labor and their faith.

It was now the 1980s and the world was changing. In 1981 Andreas Papandreou took over as Prime Minister of Greece and reduced the workweek from six to five days, a change that gave Anastasia a bit more time away from the hospital. On her days off she did shopping and visited friends in Thessaloniki. The shorter week also meant that she could leave on Saturday morning, rather than evening, for weekend visits to Mylotopos. Eastern Europe was rumbling with change. Political tensions were rising, and it was in 1985 that Anastasia and a friend made their first trip behind the Iron Curtain.

Sofia was a Greek American with a heart for visiting and supporting pastors in Communist countries. It was a dangerous time due to religious, ethnic, and military conflict, and the instability in the region escalated to the level of full-scale war during the 1990s, but Sofia was more focused on the people's need than on her personal safety. She had a car but needed a traveling companion, and Anastasia was thrilled to join her. Over the course of a year, they made nine trips to Peć and Niš, two cities in the former Yugoslavia which are now part of Kosovo and Serbia, respectively. Their purpose was to deliver much needed clothing, food, and medicine.

The majority of their visits were focused specifically on supplying two brothers, one a pastor in Peć and the other in Niš, with goods that they could not otherwise obtain. Though they were stopped several times by the police as they crossed into Peć, Sofia's American passport always gave them a green light; Yugoslavia was eager to admit foreigners who could stimulate their economy by shopping and spending American dollars. The women weren't sure what consequences they would face if they were stopped and searched, but they were never afraid. . . and their car was never inspected.

On one trip they went to see a Christian man who was the contact for a church of impoverished believers that needed clothes. They packed the car as tight as possible, filling the trunk with clothing and stuffing even more under all the seats. They slipped in and out with their precious cargo undetected. After every visit they returned to Greece with their vehicle empty and their hearts full. It was on their ninth and final trip behind the Iron Curtain, that God sowed the seeds for one of the greatest changes in Anastasia's life.

Anastasia's mother in front of their house in Greece

CHAPTER 4

A Life-Changing Proposal

In August of 1987 Anastasia attended a Bible conference in Leptokarya, Greece, on the beautiful Aegean Sea. One of the conference speakers who taught on the subject of prayer was Richard Burr, an American who had started an organization called Pray-Think-Act Ministries. Anastasia had met him two years earlier at a missions conference and appreciated his teaching. During Richard's first stay in Greece, one of the pastors at the conference thought that he might be interested in visiting St. Luke's Hospital to see the ministry there firsthand, and he enlisted Anastasia's help with lunch and a tour. Their visit culminated with prayer together in the hospital chapel. Later that week, Richard was the invited speaker at Anastasia's church in Mylotopos, and when one of the ladies invited Richard and the pastor to her home following the service, she asked Anastasia, a fluent English speaker, to join them and help facilitate communication.

Consequently, Anastasia was not surprised to see Richard again at the 1987 adult Bible conference and remembered well his previous visit. He was interested in visiting Yugoslavia and consulted with the conference organizers about the viability of a trip, but they advised that it was too dangerous. Having overheard this conversation, Anastasia spoke with the leaders and informed them of her travel plans with Sofia. It would be their ninth and final trip, and Richard was welcome to join them. The Yugoslavian pastors loved visitors from other countries and would be thrilled to meet him.

It was a bit awkward for Richard, who was single, to travel with two unmarried women, but with the blessing of the conference leadership, the three set out on a Friday morning at 4:30am. There was a bit of confusion at the border due to the demonstrations of unionized Greek workers who were on strike, but as always, God used the American passport to send their car straight through the checkpoint. The roads were primitive in comparison with highways in the West and were not in good repair even though there were fewer vehicles using them. In fact, it was very common to see oxen pulling wagons and to brake for cows that had wandered out onto the road.

The three travelers enjoyed good conversation and shared their life stories with each other as they bounced along over the bumpy roads. Riding in the front with Sofia, Richard observed that her car, a Datsun with 200,000 kilometers on the odometer, was hard to shift and didn't always have the necessary power to pass semi-trailers on the highway. She was receptive to his suggestion about downshifting and, though nothing could be done about the road conditions, that adjustment made the ride a tad smoother. They stopped briefly for a picnic lunch and then continued on to Niš.

They arrived at the pastor's home where Richard was introduced to the precautionary ruse which by now had become quite routine for the women. The family across the street was Communist and worked as informants for the government, so the pastor had developed a plan to avoid drawing unwanted attention to these deliveries. Sofia backed the car into his driveway while he raised the garage door and ushered them inside. Rather than raise suspicions by closing the door and unloading the cargo in secret, the clever pastor popped open the hood of the car and immediately took on the role of mechanic, making imaginary repairs. Meanwhile, with the hood blocking the neighbors' view, Anastasia, Sofia and Richard hurriedly unpacked the car, took all the contraband inside, and later joined the pastor and his family for a meal.

It was still early enough to make the second drop so, after a brief time of fellowship, they bid their host farewell and drove to Peć where his brother, also a pastor, lived and was under house arrest. He had been falsely accused of stealing and, although he was declared innocent after his indictment, he still continued to experience harassment. They repeated the same unloading procedure, this time in the dark, carrying some items into the house and storing others in the church building. They enjoyed a wonderful visit with the pastor and then retired to their hotel. Check-in protocol at hotels in Yugoslavia during this era was a bit unnerving; guests had to surrender their passports overnight. It was always a huge relief to have them returned to one's own possession in the morning.

The three returned to the pastor's house the following morning for a delicious breakfast of fresh feta cheese, bread, and jam and then began the 10-hour drive back to Greece. They soon realized, however, that their return trip would not be nearly as pleasant as the outgoing leg of the journey. All three became ill, and Sofia had to stop the car numerous times so they could manage their flu-like symptoms, the women heading into the fields on one side of the road while Richard crossed over to the other. Fortunately, they had a jug of water and paper towels with them to wash their hands but, much to nurse Anastasia's dismay, they had no soap. It was particularly awkward and embarrassing for Richard, the only male in the car. As their adventure came to a close and they drove back into Greece, he realized that he had never met a woman like Anastasia and he was greatly impressed by the quality of her walk with the Lord. And, it was on this trip, rough roads, stomach upset and all, that Richard sensed something happening in his heart.

The women dropped him off at the home of George and Erimone Kantartzis, an elder of the Greek Evangelical church in Katerini. An animated man who looked like Groucho Marx and spoke with his eyebrows, George's face lit up with interest and his eyebrows danced as he asked about the trip, especially Richard's impression of the two missionary women. George was unsurprised by Richard's observations about Anastasia's character and confirmed that, in his opinion, she was one of the most spiritually minded women in all the evangelical church of Greece.

Richard then went to the home of Pantelis and Roula Sidiropoulos in Thessaloniki where he would spend his final day before returning to the United States. This friendly couple invited Anastasia to join the group at an area restaurant for pizza. From the balcony where the foursome ate they basked in beauty of the Aegean Sea stretched out before them at twilight and gazed in awe at the illuminated city below. The serene ambiance was suddenly disrupted when Richard, who had stood to move his chair, accidentally kicked a spigot on the wall behind him and was drenched from the knees down by the water that sprayed out all over him and the floor. They all had a good laugh, Richard included.

As they stopped in front of Anastasia's apartment at the end of the evening, Richard exited the car with her and quickly grabbed her hand. "Let me pray with you," he said. Anastasia was deeply moved and felt something change in her heart, though she was not sure if what she was sensing was of the Lord or not. It seemed that Richard was interested in her, but, recognizing the possibility that she might never see him again, she did not want to let her mind or heart wander. Two weeks later, however, she received a letter from the United States, and reading between the lines, her suspicions were confirmed.

Meanwhile, at Sofia's urging and Anastasia's own sense that she needed a break from the intensity of her work at the hospital, the two women had already planned a trip to Canada for the fall of 1987. The Lord once again showed His generous favor and prompted the director of the hospital to offer Anastasia full pay, even during what would be a two-month leave of absence. Now, however, after correspondence with Richard in the United States, Anastasia extended the trip one additional month. Sofia had gone on ahead, and Anastasia planned to join her in Canada after a 12-day visit with Constantine, in Boston. She had spoken with Richard several times from Greece and gave him the dates when she would be with her brother.

Shortly after Anastasia's arrival in Boston, Richard called and after a few preliminary pleasantries, he was very direct with her about his intentions: "Would you be open to building a relationship with me? And, if so, and this should lead to marriage, I'm open." Anastasia was taken aback and found herself momentarily speechless, but quickly regained her composure and responded causiously, "Yes, if God so leads." Though

Richard was scheduled to be in Alberta, Canada, for several prayer conferences in November and early December, the province was so vast that it seemed unlikely they could meet in person. Sofia and Anastasia's schedule was already set, as was Richard's, and there was not much extra time, but as Anastasia traveled throughout Canada, she called him weekly.

After a few weeks, they found a way to meet in Calgary where Anastasia was staying with a nurse friend from Canada. Richard picked her up, and their first date was dinner together at a Greek restaurant. Anastasia was excited that he liked Greek food, and after a wonderful meal, he took her home. The next morning they rode up to see the Canadian Rockies. They traveled through a world of white and marveled at the sparkling glaciers and snow covered mountains. After driving all day, stopping only for meals, they reserved rooms at a hotel. They enjoyed a beautiful walk in the snow that evening, and as they strolled together for an hour or two, Richard told her even more details of his life story. He talked about his first wife and the marital challenges he had faced with an unbelieving spouse and shared his sons' stories as well. Richard did not know the Lord when he first married and started a family but came to Christ when his children were older. Tim, the eldest, was now married with children and struggled with a serious drinking and drug problem. Jeff, the middle son, was a flight attendant for United Airlines. He was a homosexual and was estranged from his father. Bruce, the youngest, was married and starting his own business in Arizona.

As Anastasia lay in her bed that night unable to sleep, the details of all that Richard had shared spun round and round in her mind. "What in the world am I doing with a man who has a story like that?" she asked herself. She spent hours in prayer seeking the Lord's will and eventually had peace in her heart.

It was snowing the next morning when Richard picked her up and drove her to the airport in Calgary. She flew to Vancouver to stay with another friend while Sofia visited friends elsewhere. Richard returned to his home in Pennsylvania, and they continued to communicate by what were now daily, rather than weekly, phone calls. Anastasia then flew to Los Angeles from where, after a short visit, she would travel to Boston. Richard suggested that she alter her plans and fly into Pittsburgh instead so she could visit New Castle, the small community in western Pennsylvania where he lived.

Their relationship was deepening, and Anastasia realized that she needed to see Richard's world up close. She stayed at the lovely Tavern Inn on the Square in nearby New Wilmington and spent three days talking with Richard, touring the area, and meeting family. She loved Richard's mother and later complimented her, "I hope when I'm your age, I'm as sweet as you are." The climax of her visit was on New Year's Eve, when as they sat under the Christmas tree at Richard's home, he proposed. It was an unforgettable moment, but Anastasia could not reply with an immediate "yes". Her response was that she needed time to think and pray. Anastasia wanted the Lord to speak to her heart and would look to Him for guidance through prayer as she had before making every major decision in her life. Richard suggested that she contact St. Luke's to extend her leave of absence, and they graciously granted her the months of January and February.

And so, in January 1988, Richard and Anastasia began a period of extensive travel throughout the eastern United States. Their first stop was her brother's home in Boston where Richard formally asked permission for Anastasia's hand in marriage. By this time, her father Christos had passed away, and Constantine served as the family patriarch. He as well as his wife and children loved Richard immediately, and he happily granted his blessing on the proposal. It was important to Anastasia that Richard meet at least part of her family, and Constantine's reaction was confirming.

She accompanied Richard to his scheduled prayer conferences during January and February, and along the way they squeezed in visits with his organization's board members and other friends. Richard wanted their input on this life-changing step and its potential impact on the ministry. They first met with John Carlson and his wife Marion in Cambridge, New York, and then passed through New York City where Anastasia met family friends and directors of Hephzibah House Ministries, John and Lois Ewald. From there, they flew to Tampa, Florida, and stayed overnight with another board member, Dr. Dick Mayer, and his wife, Bonnie. When Richard went downstairs for coffee the next morning, he asked Bonnie what she thought about Anastasia. "That's not the question, Richard," she replied with a twinkle in her eye. The question is, "Are YOU good enough for her?" They then traveled to Miami for a wonderful visit with Mac and Denise West. The unanimous affirmation of these friends and supporters and the love with which they embraced Anastasia provided additional confirmation that their plans for marriage were of God, but she had not yet heard directly from the Lord and continued to seek His clear leading.

Before flying back to Boston for one last visit with her brother en route to Greece, Anastasia gave Richard her answer. Her response was that she needed clear guidance from the Lord through His Word and that she wanted to seek the approval of her pastor and perhaps some of the elders from her church in Thessaloniki who knew both of them. By the time she arrived home, word had already spread quickly around her church community that she was going to marry. She anticipated hesitation on the part of her pastor because Richard was divorced, but before she contacted him to initiate a conversation, he called her. Much to her surprise the purpose of his call was to ask when she planned to hold the ceremony; many of the elders would be out of town on vacation during the summer and would be unavailable. Anastasia sidestepped what for her was the premature issue of dates and asked him directly, "You approve of my marriage?" His response was sincere and straightforward: "Of course. We know Richard, we know you and we know what the Bible teaches on these issues. You have my okay." Richard, who called frequently and regularly asked Anastasia where she was in the decision making process, was happy to hear the news. His hopes rose as her certainty increased with each call: "Richard, I'm 93% sure" and by the next conversation, "I'm 95% sure." Her pastor's approval marked another step forward, but Anastasia was still compelled to pray. It was the Lord's confirmation that she needed.

Anastasia wanted to be absolutely certain before moving forward and prayed that the Lord would give her a special Scripture passage that would speak to her personally. She had three specific questions with which she repeatedly went before the Lord. These were issues that had to be resolved in order for her to marry Richard. First, was her ministry in Greece over? Second, would her mother who lived all alone in their house in Mylotopos be alright without her? Her sister was willing to care for their mother because Anastasia's work schedule permitted only weekly visits, but was this the answer? And third, was this the right man for her?

One morning in her devotional reading, God spoke. His voice was unmistakable and left no room for doubt. The Scripture that He gave her addressed all three concerns. Psalm 45:10-11 (NIV): "Listen, daughter, and pay careful attention: Forget your people and your father's house. The king is enthralled by your beauty; honor him, for he is your lord." It seemed clear that the season of medical ministry to her fellow Greeks had come an end and that she was to leave her family in God's hands and marry the man who was in love with her. She was at peace, and excitedly picked up the phone to call Richard and give him her definitive answer.

After much discussion, Richard and Anastasia decided that a wedding in the United States would be less expensive and more convenient, and Anastasia flew to Boston in June where she stayed with Constantine until the ceremony. Planning an American wedding was quite an undertaking, but God provided in unique ways. Heeding the advice of the Joey and Jim Steele, whom they had visited in Indiana, Richard and Anastasia stopped at a Laura Ashley Outlet Store in Columbus, Ohio, to look for a wedding dress. The first dress she tried was gorgeous . . . and it fit perfectly. They paid $250 for a $1,500 gown. Richard had always been attracted to his fiancée's fine character, and he was overwhelmed by her outward beauty as well.

The wedding was held on August 13, 1988, in a small chapel at Hephzibah Heights Conference Center in Monterey, Massachusetts, the Berkshire Mountains counterpart to the New

York City Hephzibah ministry. Their transportation to the chapel was memorable: Richard picked up Anastasia at her cottage in a golf cart! It was a beautiful summer day, and about 80 people gathered to celebrate with the new couple. John and Lois' teenage daughter, Jennifer, served as Anastasia's bridesmaid, and two pastor friends, John Carlson and David McDowell, performed a lovely ceremony. Richard and Anastasia were surrounded by many loved ones, including Constantine and his family, and following the service, enjoyed a wonderful dinner reception with their guests. They both shared their testimonies and retold their love story emphasizing the solid foundation of prayer on which their marriage was established. Anastasia was 44 years old and Richard was 56 when they took this new step, and they had no doubt that this was God's will at this particular point in their lives. After a brief honeymoon in Vermont, the Burrs took up residence on Garfield Avenue in New Castle, Pennsylvania, and began their new life together.

Anastasia in 2003 when she became a U.S. citizen

CHAPTER 5

Ministry in the United States

For Anastasia, accustomed to Thessaloniki with a population of one million, moving to New Castle, a city of approximately 25,000 people, was like falling off the end of the earth. It took a bit of adjustment, but knowing in her heart that God had led her brought a deep sense of peace. Richard had canceled all his conferences for August and September to give the newlyweds a month or so to adapt to their new life. This period of transition was sadly interrupted by the sudden death of his mother on September 20th. It was almost as if, humanly speaking, Mother Burr had waited until her son was married, and knowing that he was in caring hands, let go. They grieved together the passing of this godly woman, but their mourning was intermingled with the certainty that she was with her Savior.

They started on the road to their first conference, unsure of how the many churches with which Richard worked would receive his new wife. Though the reception at their first church in Massachusetts was positive, the experience was more adventurous than they might have expected. They always lodged with a member of the host church, and their first overnight stay was especially memorable. They slept in a double bed with a mattress that must have dated from Massachusetts' colonial days: its squishy sink hole in the middle forced them either to clutch their respective sides or release their grip and roll to the center of the bed. Needless to say, they did not sleep. To make matters worse, someone broke into their car in the parking lot on the first night of the conference and stole their luggage while Richard was speaking. They reported the incident to the police, and the thieves were never found, but amazingly, Richard and Anastasia did manage to recover a few of their belongings . . . and in a most unlikely way. The next day as they headed for the church, they noticed a piece of cloth with a familiar print dangling from a bush on the side of the road: Richard's pajamas! They stopped to reclaim them. Continuing on, they found more of their personal effects strewn along the road, including Richard's underwear and Anastasia's hair dryer, etc. Their life together on the road was off to an unforgettable start.

Looking back, they wondered if perhaps taking the first six months of their marriage to get to know each another before hitting the road would have been wise. Nevertheless, Anastasia remembers floating in the grace of God and adjusting fairly quickly to life in the United States, never feeling overcome by homesickness or loneliness. Having already lived in two English-speaking countries, her language skills were excellent, though the regional idioms of Southern English sometimes presented a challenge. She stayed in frequent contact with her family by phone and drew special strength from the Word of God during those months of transition. Her personal prayer life put into the practice the principles that she heard Richard teach regularly at the conferences.

PTAM stands for Pray-Think-Act Ministries. It was founded in 1982 as a ministry of prayer, focused specifically on the secret closet of prayer referenced in Matthew 6:6 (NIV): "But when you pray, go into your room, close the door and pray to your Father, who is unseen. Then your Father, who sees what is done in secret, will reward you." Whether it be in daily devotions or confronting the challenging situations in life, believers must pray, think about the Word, and then act on the Word's teaching. This secret closet, praying effectively in solitude with God, is a concept and a practice that is lacking in today's church. As Richard traveled the country he found that most believers had never experienced this reality, and it was their unfamiliarity with the practice that made the seminars exciting. People responded enthusiastically, and the Burrs received many letters over the years from scores of individuals who wanted to express their gratitude for the ministry. They saw that Scripture praying is a very powerful practice in developing a private prayer life because it keeps one grounded in the will of God and is the launch pad of personal revival.

The conferences were held at evangelical churches of all different persuasions and in many states across the country. It was a blessed life—sometimes tiring but God always gave strength and encouragement. Richard was the primary presenter and gave seminars nightly from Sunday through Wednesday. Anastasia felt that the Lord had prepared her in a special way for her role in encouraging and supporting Richard. Her personal revival at the conference for medical workers in Holland years before after a dry season in her own life served as a constant and vivid reminder of the centrality of prayer. Her gift for languages also proved to be a great support in several ways. Though English was not her first language, she was a strong editor and had a sharp eye for catching an occasional grammar error in the written materials. Her knowledge of Greek was also invaluable, and Richard would frequently refer to her as his "living Greek lexicon." A second way she supported the ministry was by speaking to women. It was a privilege for her to share her testimony and encourage them to develop deep, rich prayer lives.

Anastasia's intimate walk with God spilled over into a series of thoughtful poems written in the early 1990s and published by PTAM in 2012. She wrote about the foundational elements of a believer's walk such as redemption, restoration, the practice of prayer, faithful service, comfort in the midst of sorrow, and the joyful anticipation of Christ's second coming. Communicating basic information in one's second language can be a challenge, but the Lord enabled Anastasia to articulate deep spiritual truths in English and express them in beautiful poetic form.

The Burrs' faith was challenged in new ways during the 1990s. While they were at a conference in Nebraska in 1991, they received word that Anastasia's mother had died, and it was in January 1995 that Anastasia herself began experiencing several disturbing symptoms. She felt ill, and her pulse was extremely high. The doctor concluded it was anxiety, but she did not take any medication for eight months and consequently

Anastasia and Richard while attending his high school reunion in 2000.

fell into a deep depression. Over the years, she discovered that many believers struggled with depression and anxiety, and she learned to understand and identify with them.

At the same time in 1995, they sold their house in New Castle and spent the next 18 months staying in other people's homes as they pressed on with the ministry. During that time Anastasia continued to struggle with anxiety and depression and was beginning to feel desperate for a home of any kind to call their own. They waited on the Lord; they had never asked for support, apart from the beginning of PTAM, and would not start now. They trusted God completely to provide for every need.

After much prayer, Richard and Anastasia watched the providence of God intervene miraculously in their lives through what seemed to be a routine exchange over the phone. During a conversation with a pastor friend who had called just to touch base, Richard mentioned in passing that he and Anastasia were looking either for a house or for a plot where they could build one. Interestingly, this friend's house was for sale, and he invited the Burrs to take a look. They drove out with much excitement to tour the property, but their high hopes were quickly dashed when they realized that due to the age of the house, it would be extremely expensive to renovate. The Lord, however, was not finished orchestrating their circumstances. When they declined to buy his house, this dear brother responded, "Well, would you like the acre next to it? It's yours for a token." They wholeheartedly accepted the generous offer. They received an amazing answer to prayer, a dear friend as a neighbor, a basically free one-acre lot, and, subsequently, generous discounts from a Christian contractor who built a new home that fit their budget. They were continually amazed by the faithfulness and the provision of God.

On December 1, 1995, a group of friends carried the Burrs' belongings from storage into their new house in New Wilmington, Pennsylvania, a town of approximately 2,500 people located about 10 miles from their previous location. A quaint, largely rural community, it is home to Westminster College and is surrounded by the farms of some 1,500 Amish families, the third largest old order sect in the United States. The Burrs lived in a beautiful area and were blessed with a place to rest and rejuvenate between travels.

By August 1995, Anastasia had begun taking medication for anxiety and depression. She noticed a significant difference after just two weeks and praised God for giving wisdom to the scientists who had developed such life-changing medications, but by the time they moved into their new home, the positive effects wore off. She entered into what would be a cyclical pattern of trying new pills and consulting with different doctors every few months in search of a permanent solution. In trying to manage some gastrointestinal symptoms that year, she based her diet largely on baby food, and her doctor was extremely concerned to see her weight drop from a healthy 110 pounds to barely 90. He encouraged her to eat more heartily and treat herself to an occasional steak dinner, but dietary changes did not have a lasting effect.

As Anastasia continued to pray through these health issues, she and Richard suddenly found themselves confronted with another crisis. During their courtship, he had shared with her about several challenging family situations, and when they married, Anastasia partnered with him in prayer to take those issues before the throne of grace. Now, years later, a phone call out of the blue from their youngest son, Bruce, brought them once again to their knees: their second son, Jeff, was in the hospital in Denver dying of AIDS. It was Friday, October 29, 1999, a moment frozen in time.

Richard and Anastasia flew into action, cancelling travel arrangements for an early morning departure to western Canada for several conferences, and instead raced to the airport where by the grace of God they caught that evening's last flight to Denver. Though Richard had spoken with his son in recent years, it had been an agonizing decade and a half since they had seen each other. Uncertain of the reception that would await them at the hospital, Richard and Anastasia prayed fervently on the plane for a special measure of strength and grace and for wisdom as they discussed several possible scenarios, including the option of bringing Jeff home to Pennsylvania.

The Lord did not delay in answering the cries of these praying parents. As they entered Jeff's hospital room, he greeted Richard with tears of joy, a warm embrace and a repeated, "I love you, Dad—I'm so sorry," words that the father of a prodigal so longs to hear. Their Heavenly Father had heard their pleas, and the reunion was sweet. The doctor's briefing, however, was much more sobering. There was no cure for Jeff's condition. The doctors hoped to extend his life by means of blood products that would stabilize his condition and enable him to relocate to a hospice center, but that was the only medical option.

Richard and Anastasia immediately gave each other a knowing glance and almost simultaneously blurted out an invitation for Jeff to join them in Pennsylvania rather than go to a local hospice; they would love for him to spend his final days with them. Jeff was stunned. Anastasia, the second mother that he had just met for the first time, was a nurse and wanted to care for him. She did not hold his past against him nor was she repulsed by his symptoms and the stigma of his illness. Years

Anastasia and Richard in front of their home in New Wilmington, Pennsylvania

of intercessions opened her heart to a son she did not know, and she embraced the opportunity of ministering to his physical needs with compassion. Jeff enthusiastically accepted the invitation--he was loved and he knew it.

Richard and Anastasia began making logistical arrangements for the move and imagining all the ways they could saturate his final days with love, but their plans were cut short that Sunday afternoon by a devastating update from the medical team. Jeff had taken a turn for the worse, and death was imminent. Richard and Anastasia struggled to control their emotions as they spoke with him about the disappointing change of earthly plans but, even more importantly, about his preparation for eternity. Richard then had the privilege of leading his son through the process of making peace with God. Surrounded by family, Jeff uttered a simple but heartfelt prayer of repentance and confession of faith in Jesus Christ, and his loved ones were amazed by the transformation that took place before their very eyes. There was an immediate change of disposition as this dying young man, now full of joy and peace, began to express his eagerness to see Jesus. And, just one short day later, Jeff did. His newfound faith had become sight.

That unforgettable weekend in Denver was both heartbreaking and exhilarating. It was a vivid reminder of the providence of God and His gracious response to the prayers of His children. Anastasia had joined the Burr family without meeting all of its members, and God sovereignly orchestrated her introduction to son Jeffrey at the moment of his most dire medical need when she, a nurse, could offer care that no other Burr was equipped to give. It was another divine appointment in a life saturated by prayer. She and Richard grieved the painful loss and fixed their hearts in hopeful anticipation on the coming heavenly reunion where their fellowship with Jeffrey will continue uninterrupted for all of eternity.

Meanwhile, Anastasia's own health situation continued to worsen. After battling her own symptoms for years and bouncing from one doctor to another looking for help, she was relieved when, in 2009, Dr. Mark Miller at the University of Pittsburgh Medical Center did a SPECT (single-photon emission computed tomography) scan of her brain and found the answer to over a decade of physical struggle. All those years, Anastasia had been suffering from the early stages of Fronto-temporal Degeneration (FTD). FTD is a degenerative brain disorder that gradually damages the frontal and temporal lobes of the brain. Dr. Miller brought in Dr. Lopez, the head neurologist, to assist with Anastasia's care.

At 64 years of age, in late 2009, Anastasia found it very difficult to function at home and was admitted for diagnostic testing at a hospital in Pittsburgh. After a few weeks, her medical team strongly suggested that she be moved to an assisted living facility instead of returning home. She currently resides in a facility in New Wilmington where Richard is able to visit multiple times a day. Her home away from home has become another opportunity for ministry. She attributes the peace that she had in her heart from the day of the diagnosis to a miracle of God and has been able to share with others about her Savior. But, perhaps her greatest testimony during this phase of her journey is simply the presence of God flowing through her. Through days of being alone in her room she has felt the nearness of the Lord and has a desire in her heart to see Jesus more than ever before. She prays, "Lord Jesus, come quickly." At the same time He floods her heart with songs and melodies that keep her singing all day long. A few years ago she lost her physical singing voice, but the songs continue to ring out quietly within her heart.

Living apart is hard for a married couple, and the Burrs keep their relationship a priority by spending time together daily. Richard is a committed, loving husband who happily makes the short trek to see Anastasia daily in spite of many health challenges of his own. Heart and lung issues, shoulder problems, knee replacements, and multiple bouts with cancer, including, most recently, frequent surgeries for recurring malignancies in his thigh, have brought a myriad of physicians and specialists into Richard's circle of friends. Ironically, his determination to visit the love of his life regardless of his own physical trials has left a unique mark at the care facility.

One Sunday morning Richard decided to squeeze in a visit with Anastasia before the 11:00am service at church. He walked up to her second floor room where they followed their regular routine of sharing, prayer, and Scripture reading. When he headed back to the car at 10:30, he noticed that an ambulance had parked directly behind him and was blocking his car. After waiting a few minutes, he reentered the building and scanned the lobby and hallways for some sign of the ambulance driver but saw no one. The minutes passed and Richard grew a bit impatient. It was now 10:50. He went inside again and looked around, but the driver was still nowhere in sight.

Now the clock was really ticking, and Richard was going to be late for church. After one last glance around, he opened the driver's side door of the ambulance and spotted the keys in the ignition. If he backed the ambulance up just a few short feet, he would easily be able to get his own car out. He quickly slipped into the driver's seat, released the brake, shifted into reverse, and, accompanied by the loud, rhythmical "beep," "beep," "beep" of the back-up alert system, slowly eased the ambulance back. "There, that should do it," he thought, just before feeling a very slight bump. He must have nudged the stack of wooden chairs that he saw in the side-view mirror. He hopped into his car, pulled it out of its spot and then re-boarded the ambulance to re-park it in its original position. He arrived at church just in the knick of time.

Later that week, the maintenance superintendent knocked on Anastasia's door while Richard was visiting. "Hi, Dick!" Richard exclaimed, "what can I do for you?" The man was obviously uncomfortable and hesitantly poked his head inside the door to ask if they could speak in the hallway. "Come on in here," Richard replied. "It's no problem." The reluctant employee entered and began to ask Richard a series of questions. Did he drive a white car? Yes. Had he visited Anastasia on Sunday? Yes. Had he moved an ambulance in the parking lot? Well, yes, but only after waiting quite a while. Had he hit anything with the ambulance? Oh, yes, he did bump that stack of wooden chairs.

Still completely unaware of what was going on, Richard

followed Dick outside and was stunned by what he saw. One of the two structural columns that sustain the overhang just outside the entrance to the building was severely damaged. He hadn't hit a stack of chairs but had backed into a support pillar! Dick proceeded to explain that the facility had filed a police report for the property damage and that driving an ambulance without authorization was a felony violation. A white car had been spotted at the scene of the incident; they had looked for it to no avail until someone remembered that Anastasia's husband drove a car that fit the description.

And so, shaking like a leaf, this minister of the gospel who illegally drove an emergency vehicle and then fled like a hit-and-run driver from the scene of an accident, walked sheepishly into the office of the executive director of Anastasia's care facility to explain and to apologize and offer to pay for the damage. The director graciously accepted his apology. She asked several questions about his medications and was not surprised to hear that he was taking strong painkillers for a surgery he had undergone the week prior. She concluded their conversation with a smile and gentle rebuke: "That Mr. Burr is precisely why we do not allow our residents to drive while on medication."

To this day Richard cannot explain his presumptuous actions, whether the effect of his own strong medications or just an overpowering bout of impatience, but his embarrassment over the situation turned to hearty laughter when son Bruce mailed him an honorary certificate of completion for an Ambulance Driver Course along with a mini toy ambulance to commemorate the experience.

Living in a care facility can be difficult and, as Anastasia reflects on her life, she testifies that the sovereignty of God is the characteristic that most stands out and that keeps her from complaining about her illness. He could have prevented it but has allowed it for a purpose. She cites the story of Job as just one example of a person who, in the midst of severe trials, found comfort in Jesus Christ and in the sovereignty of God (Job 19:25-27). She daily fixes her mind on His power and authority to work all things for the good of those that love Him, thereby ordaining whatever comes to pass. She feels His love, experiences His compassion, and knows firsthand His faithfulness. Her illness causes terrible tremors and her hands now shake so severely that she can no longer write her name, but she trusts that God is in control.

From those early days on Grandmother's lap in Greece to her room at a care facility in western Pennsylvania, every season of Anastasia's life has been saturated with prayer. Whether in Turkish, Greek or English, she has consistently sought the face of God, and by His good providence He has directed her path for over 70 years. Her story is full of preordained details and divinely orchestrated circumstances that stretched her faith in new and deeper ways with each passing year. She trusted Him for the courage to leave her family and country in faithful obedience to His call. She trusted Him to pay every tuition expense, open the door for nurses' training, and provide strength to love every patient. She trusted Him to open hearts at the hospital to the Gospel. She trusted Him to slip her undetected behind the Iron Curtain. She trusted Him to reveal through His Word if the marriage proposal set before her was of Him. She trusted Him for journey mercies during 20 plus years of ministry travel with Richard and for the funds to meet their needs month by month. She trusted Him with her diagnosis of FTD and her move away from home for care.

Tracing the path of God's providential work in the past provides a sure foundation of faith for the future. The loving Heavenly Father who has answered Anastasia's every prayer and guided her every step will continue to do so. By God's grace, she lives one day at a time in fellowship with the Savior and endures the cross of momentary affliction with her eyes firmly fixed on the unseen glory that awaits her in her eternal Home. Those who know her personally are confident that she will hear, "Well done, good and faithful servant" (Matthew 25:23).